Healing Your Inner Child

Healing Your Inner Child

A Guided Workbook for Healing the Wounds of Childhood Trauma

Disclaimer: This workbook is for educational and informational purposes only and is not a substitute for therapy, medical care, diagnosis, or treatment. Reading this book and completing the exercises does not create a therapist-client relationship. If you are experiencing significant distress, worsening symptoms, or feel unable to keep yourself safe, seek professional support in your area.

Publisher: Courageous Journeys®

Contact: connect@courageousjourneys.com

ISBN (paperback): 978-1-7360508-9-7

First edition: 2026

Dedication

For the child you were and the adult who continues to unfold into all you were meant to be.

May this workbook meet you with grounded trust in your strength and capacity to heal.

May it help you remember what has always been true beneath the pain, fear, and doubt.

May it make space for comfort, clarity, and the freedom you've always deserved.

To my courageous community, thank you. Thank you for trusting me with your hope and stories of pain, resilience, courage, and joy. Thank you for allowing me to walk alongside you and witness your becoming.

Contents

Welcome to Your Journey of Reconnecting and Healing the Child Within

A note before we begin

Take a moment to notice how you're feeling right now. Are you hopeful? Nervous? Maybe a little skeptical? All these feelings are natural and welcome. There's no right way to feel as you navigate this journey.

You're holding this workbook because something inside you knows healing is possible. Not just managing symptoms or coping better, but genuine freedom from the wounds that have shaped how you see yourself and move through the world. That knowing, that inner voice that brought you here, it's worth trusting.

What this workbook is (and what it's not)

This isn't another self-help book that promises quick fixes, tells you to "just think positive", or suggests that by following these steps you'll be healed.

This is a companion for real work; the kind that happens slowly, with patience, and with deep respect for your experiences.

You won't find trendy terminology or complicated theories here. Instead, you'll find practices, exercises, and gentle guidance designed to help you connect with the parts of yourself that learned to survive in ways that may create difficulty for you now. The child who developed these survival strategies was brilliant and resourceful. Now it's time to help that child heal and feel *truly* safe and free.

This workbook can be used on its own or alongside therapy. It's designed to be returned to again and again. Healing happens in layers, moment by moment. Some days you might feel ready to dive deep, other days you might just need a gentle reminder that you're not alone in this. Both are natural and part of the journey.

Your inner child: A different way of understanding

When we talk about your "inner child", we're not talking about a concept or metaphor. We're talking about the very real parts of you that were shaped by your earliest experiences; the parts that learned what love looked like, what safety felt like, and what you needed to do to survive.

For many of us, what we learned about love and safety as children wasn't actually love or safety at all. It may have been conditional, unpredictable, or even harmful. But it became our blueprint for what we believed about how the world works.

That child isn't broken, damaged, or at fault. That child is the part of you that holds your capacity for joy, creativity, wonder, and authentic connection. That child may also be carrying pain, fear, and beliefs that impact their sense of self and what is possible for them in the world.

Think of it this way: if you met a child who experienced what you experienced, you wouldn't tell them to "get over it" or "move on." You'd want to understand their experience, validate their feelings, and help them feel safe. You'd meet them with compassion, not judgment or blame.

This workbook will help you offer that same compassion to yourself.

It's also important to recognize that your inner child may be any age from newborn to adulthood. With each additional traumatic experience through childhood, the earlier beliefs and fears are reinforced, becoming more ingrained.

I sometimes use "little one" for exercises and practices, if this doesn't resonate, choose a name, word, or phrase that does. There is no right or wrong, it just needs to be something you can feel connected to.

What you can expect

This journey will guide you to:

- Look at your story with honesty and compassion
- Feel feelings that may have been buried for years
- Challenge beliefs about yourself that feel like absolute truth
- Practice new ways of relating to yourself and others
- Be patient with a process that doesn't follow a timeline

This journey will offer you:

- A deeper understanding of why you think, feel, and respond the way you do
- Tools for connecting with yourself in moments of pain or struggle
- Practices for releasing shame and responsibility that were never yours to carry
- A sense of genuine compassion for your own experience
- Glimpses of the freedom that comes from healing, not just coping

How to use this workbook

There's no perfect way to do this work. Some people will move through it section by section. Others will jump around based on what feels relevant. Some will fill every blank. Others will use it more as a guide for their own reflection. There is extra space at the end to allow yourself to explore your thoughts and reactions through journaling, drawing, or doodling.

Recommendations as you go through the journey:

- **Go at your own pace**. This isn't a race. If something feels too intense, slow down or take a break.
- **Write in the margins**. Make this workbook yours. Add your own thoughts, questions, and insights.
- **Return to exercises**. Your responses will likely evolve as you move through the healing process.
- **Practice self-compassion**. If you notice yourself being critical or judgmental, pause and ask: "How would I speak to a child or someone else I cared about?"
- **Seek support when needed**. This work can bring up intense emotions. Having a therapist, trusted friend, or support group can be invaluable.

A word about emotional safety

Healing from childhood wounds can sometimes feel overwhelming. As you work through these exercises, you might experience:

- Intense emotions or memories
- Physical sensations or reactions
- Feeling more vulnerable or sensitive than usual
- Temporary increases in anxiety or sadness

This is normal, but it's important to take care of yourself. If you find yourself feeling overwhelmed, notice you're not coping well, or find yourself isolating, please reach out for professional support. None of us can heal completely on our own. And remember, this journey is about healing the part of you that depends on you to continue to show up for yourself and them.

The courage that brought you here

It may not seem like it but, simply opening this workbook takes courage. Deciding to look at your story, to feel your feelings, to consider that healing is possible, these are acts of strength and bravery.

You might not feel strong or brave right now. You might feel scared, overwhelmed, or unsure. That's okay. Courage isn't the absence of fear; it's the decision to move forward when you're uncertain or afraid.

The child in you who survived whatever you survived was incredibly strong. That same strength is available to you now and can be used for healing instead of simply surviving.

Before you begin

Take a moment to set an intention for this journey. It doesn't have to be profound or perfectly worded. It just needs to be true for you.

Maybe it's something like:

- *I want to understand myself better*
- *I want to feel less alone in my experience*
- *I want to stop being so hard on myself*
- *I want to feel free from my past*

My intention for this healing journey:

Something to keep in mind

While I may not know you personally, I want you to know that every word in this workbook comes from a place of deep respect for your experience, courage, and resilience and an unshakeable belief in your capacity to heal. You are not broken. You are not too damaged. You are not beyond hope.

You are a person who experienced things that no child should have to experience, and you survived. Now you have the opportunity to do more than survive, you have the opportunity to reconnect and heal all the parts of yourself that have been wounded and possibly left behind.

Your story matters. Your feelings matter. You matter.

And most importantly - you deserve to be free.

Ready? Let's begin.

Part 1 - Understanding Your Story

Before we dive in, let's take a moment to connect with where you are right now. Take a deep breath. Notice how your body feels in this moment. Are you tense anywhere? Relaxed? Just notice, without trying to change anything.

You're here because something inside you knows that healing is possible. That's your power. It takes courage to look at our stories, especially the parts that hurt. I want you to know from the start: you're not broken, and you don't need to be fixed. You need to be seen, understood, and cared for, starting with how you see and care for all the parts of yourself.

Your experience matters

When we talk about childhood trauma or wounding, we're not *just* talking about the "big" things that might come to mind: abuse, neglect, or obvious harm. We're talking about any experience that taught you, as a child, that you weren't safe, weren't valued, or weren't enough exactly as you were. Even if that learning was subconscious. Sometimes, especially when that learning was subconscious.

Maybe it was a parent who was physically there but emotionally unavailable. Maybe it was being told you were "too much" or "too sensitive." Maybe it was having to grow up too fast, taking care of adults who should have been taking care of you. Maybe it was experiencing racism, discrimination, violence, or uncertainty in your community. Maybe it was having your feelings dismissed or being told to "get over it." Maybe it was not having enough... love, attention, resources, or connection. Or, simply, a belief you were not enough or deserving.

It doesn't matter if you think other people had it "worse." It doesn't matter if your parents or those around you "did their best." What matters is that a child... you... experienced something that left a mark.

Take a moment: What comes up for you when you read those words? Notice any thoughts, feelings, or sensations in your body. Don't judge them, just notice.

Space for reflection:

The child who lived it

It's natural to look back at experiences and think you should have thought, felt, or done something differently. It's also natural to automatically think that in those childhood moments you should have had all the awareness and understanding you do now.

This is where so much of the sense of responsibility and shame are reinforced. Whether it's asking yourself why you did or didn't do something you think would have changed things or berating or judging yourself for not being able to stop it, change it, or feeling or thinking the way you do.

When we talk about your childhood experiences and your inner child, we're not talking about the adult you looking back, the adult you that has agency, power, and awareness. We're talking about an actual child who lived through these things with no autonomy or ability to create change.

Think for a moment about a child you know, or even just picture a child who's the same age you were when something difficult happened to you. Really try to imagine that child in your mind. How big are they? What do they look like when they're happy? What do they look like when they're scared or hurt?

That child you're picturing deserves love, protection, and care, right? Of course they do. They deserve to have their feelings validated, their needs met, and their worth celebrated.

This might feel hard to take in but, you were that child. You deserved all those things too.

Journal Prompt: Write about yourself as a child at a specific age (pick any age that feels significant to you). Describe what you looked like, what you enjoyed, what made you laugh, what scared or worried you? Write about this child with the same tenderness you'd have for any child you cared about. You might even consider finding a picture of yourself around that age to try to reconnect.

Space for writing:

How it shows up now

Childhood experiences don't just stay in the past, they live in our bodies, our thoughts, our patterns, and our deeply held beliefs. This isn't a character flaw and it's not weakness. It's how we're wired as humans.

Maybe you find yourself:

- Feeling like you're not enough, no matter what you accomplish
- Having a hard time trusting people or getting close to others
- Feeling responsible for everyone else's feelings
- Struggling with anxiety, depression, or feeling overwhelmed
- Having a critical inner voice that never seems to quiet down
- Feeling like you're always waiting for the other shoe to drop
- People-pleasing to avoid conflict or rejection
- Feeling guilty when you try to take care of yourself

Body Check-In: As you read that list, what do you notice in your body? Take a few deep breaths and scan from the top of your head down to your toes. Are there areas of tension? Heaviness? Tightness? Just notice without trying to change anything.

What I noticed:

The stories we tell ourselves

As humans, we're meaning-making beings. As children, our ability t by our much smaller pool of experiences along with where we are de something bad happens, we don't think "this adult is having a proble about me." We create stories to make sense of our experiences, and beliefs we carry about ourselves, others, and the world around us.

Some common stories might sound like:

- *I'm too much*
- *I'm bad*
- *I'm not lovable*
- *I can't trust anyone*
- *I have to be perfect to be worthy of love*
- *My feelings don't matter... I don't matter*
- *I'm responsible for everyone else's happiness*
- *If I'm good enough, maybe they'll love me... maybe they'll pro*

These stories made sense to a child trying to survive. They might have some ways. But they're not the truth about who you are. *They never ha*

Reflection Exercise: What stories about yourself do you think you le worry about getting it "right", just notice what comes up.

Stories I learned about myself:

rned about others:

arned about the world:

me game

e telling you this right now isn't going to make you magically believe it but, none of ful experiences were your fault. Not the trauma, not the neglect, not the ways you were t down. Nothing about what happened to you was your fault.

ur mind might be jumping in with "but what about when I..." or "if I hadn't been so... ." e a breath.

Remember that child you pictured earlier? If they came to you and told you about experiencing what you experienced, would you tell them it was their fault? Would you tell them they should have known better, done something different, been less difficult?

Of course you wouldn't. Because you know, deep down, that children don't cause the harm that happens to them. They don't deserve it, they don't ask for it, and they can't prevent it.

You were and are no different than that child. The same truth applies to you. *It always has.*

Practice: Place one hand on your heart and one on your belly. Take three deep breaths, exhaling for a count longer than the inhale. With each exhale, imagine releasing just a tiny bit of the blame or responsibility you've been carrying. You don't have to let it all go right now, just see if you can soften around it, even slightly.

What comes up when you try this practice:

Moving forward

This is just the beginning. Understanding your story, really understanding it from a place of compassion and objectivity, not judgment, is the foundation for everything that comes next.

You might notice that reading this section brings up a lot of feelings. That's normal. You might feel sad, angry, relieved, or even numb. All these responses are okay. Healing isn't linear, and it's rarely comfortable. Healing is a process and through the process you will likely feel a variety of feelings. Sometimes seemingly all at once or nothing at all.

A promise to yourself: Before we move on, I invite you to make a commitment to yourself. It doesn't have to be huge, just something that honors your willingness to be here, doing this work. Keep in mind that this is not about perfection. It's about honoring yourself and your healing.

My commitment to myself as I begin this journey:

Daily Practice: For the next week, I encourage you to practice seeing yourself as that child, just once a day. It might be when you look in the mirror, when you make a mistake, or when you're being hard on yourself. Remember - you're seeing a child who deserved love and care. How might you speak to yourself differently?

Space for daily notes:

Remember: This workbook is meant to be returned to. Don't feel like you need to "get it right" the first time through. Healing happens in layers, and each time you revisit these exercises, you might discover something new.

Part 2 - Connecting with Compassion

If you've made it this far, you're already doing something many people haven't. You've opened yourself up. You've stepped into vulnerability. You're willing to push through denial or avoidance to look at your story from a new, more gentle perspective; recognizing that an actual child lived through these experiences. That takes courage.

Now comes what might be the most important part of this entire journey: learning to connect with that child, not just intellectually, but with your whole heart. This isn't about analyzing what happened or figuring out how to fix it. This is about showing up for the child you were with the same kind of presence you'd offer any child who needed comfort.

Before we begin, let's check in with your body. Take a slow breath in through your nose, hold it for just a moment, then let it out through your mouth. Notice if and where you're holding tension. Are your shoulders up by your ears? Is your jaw clenched? Were you holding your breath before the cue to breathe? Just breathe into those spaces and see if you can soften, even slightly.

Understanding compassion

When I talk about compassion, I'm not talking about self-pity or feeling sorry for yourself or "wallowing" in what happened. I'm not even talking about letting yourself off the hook for *real* mistakes you may have made in your life. I'm talking about the kind of warm, steady presence you'd offer to any child or someone you care about who was hurting.

Think about how you naturally respond when you see a child who's scared or sad. You don't lecture them about why they shouldn't feel that way. You don't tell them to get over it or that it's not a big deal. You get down on their level, you listen, you validate their experience, and you offer comfort.

That's compassion. It's not soft or weak, it's actually incredibly strong. It says "I see you, I believe you, and you're not alone."

Reflection: Think of a time when someone showed you genuine compassion, maybe a friend, teacher, or even a stranger. How did it feel to be seen and cared for without judgment? If nothing comes to mind right now, imagine what it would feel like.

What I remember about receiving compassion:

The "other child" practice

This can be a powerful experience. It can also bring up some emotion. Please stay mindful as you go through this practice. Maybe consider a grounding practice before continuing. Remember, it's okay to take a break if needed or come back to this exercise another time.

Think of a child in your life, maybe a niece, nephew, a friend's child, or even just a child you might see at the grocery store. If you can't think of a specific child, just imagine a child who's the same age you were when something difficult happened to you.

Now, imagine that child coming to you and sharing ***your*** story. They tell you about the same experiences you had, the same hurt, the same fear, the same confusion, the same beliefs about themselves. They look up at you with eyes that are hoping someone will understand.

What would you say to that child? How would you hold them? What would your voice sound like? What would you want them to know?

Writing Exercise: Write a letter to this child as if they just told you your story. Let your natural compassion flow.

Dear Little One,

Take a moment... take this in... you deserve that same response. The child you were deserves those same words, that same care, that same validation. There's nothing different about you that makes you less deserving of compassion, care, concern, or support. Truly, there isn't.

Body Practice: Place both hands on your heart, right over left. Close your eyes if that feels comfortable. Take three deep breaths. With each breath, imagine offering yourself even a tiny bit of the compassion you just wrote about. You don't have to believe it completely, just practice the gesture.

What comes up when I try to offer myself compassion:

____

____

____

____

____

____

Meeting your younger self

This next exercise might feel strange at first but stay with me. I want you to imagine meeting yourself as a child. Not thinking about your childhood, actually meeting that child as if they were standing right in front of you. Notice what you... or they, might need afterward and try to create space and opportunity to meet that need.

Guided Visualization:

Allow yourself to be in a comfortable, quiet space in a position that will allow your body to relax.

Close your eyes and take a few deep breaths. Picture yourself in a place that feels safe and comfortable, maybe a cozy room, a beautiful garden, or somewhere that feels peaceful. Maybe it's a real place you've experienced, either as a child or adult, or it can be someplace you create in your mind.

Now imagine that into this safe space walks you as a child. Pick an age that feels significant, maybe when something difficult happened, or just an age that comes to mind. Really see this child. Notice what they're wearing, how they're standing, what their expression looks like.

This child has been waiting a long time to be seen... to be felt by you. They've been carrying so much, trying so hard to be good enough, to figure out how to be safe and loved.

If it feels right, imagine approaching this child slowly. You might sit down so you're at their level. You might smile gently. You might simply say "I see you." or "I'm here." Maybe even "You're safe."

Notice what this child needs from you right now. Maybe they need to hear that what happened wasn't their fault. Maybe they need to know they're loved exactly as they are. Maybe they just need someone to sit with them.

Trust whatever comes up. This child knows what they need.

Spend a few minutes just being present with this younger version of yourself. You don't have to say anything profound or fix anything. Your presence is enough.

When you're ready, you might let this child know that you're not going anywhere. That you're going to learn how to take better care of them. That they're not alone anymore.

Take a few more deep breaths, and when you're ready, open your eyes.

Journal Reflection: What was this experience like for you? What did you notice about your younger self? What did they seem to need? What sensations do you notice in your body?

What I noticed about meeting my younger self:

What this child seemed to need from me:

What I notice in my body:

Understanding your protective patterns

As you start to connect with your younger self, you might notice some resistance. Maybe your mind says things like "This is silly" or "I don't have time for this" or "I need to focus on real problems." Maybe you feel uncomfortable with the vulnerability of it all.

Whatever you notice, it's okay. Actually, it's more than okay, it's helpful information.

The parts of you that resist this work are often the same parts that have been trying to protect you all along. They developed strategies to keep you safe, to help you survive, to prevent you from being hurt again.

Maybe you learned to:

- Stay busy so you don't have to feel
- Be perfect so you (hopefully) won't be criticized
- Take care of everyone else so you feel valuable
- Keep people at a distance so you won't be abandoned
- Minimize your own needs so you're not a burden or can stay hidden

These patterns served a purpose. They helped you make it through. And the parts of you that developed them deserve acknowledgment, not judgment.

Reflection: What patterns or strategies do you think you developed to protect yourself? What has your mind/body/heart been trying to keep you safe from?

Some ways I learned to protect myself:

What these patterns were trying to protect me from:

Honoring all your feelings

One of the most important things you can do for your younger self is to let them feel everything they need to feel. Children who experience trauma or chronic difficulties often learn that their feelings are too much, too inconvenient, too dangerous, or simply don't matter.

Maybe you learned that anger wasn't safe, so you pushed it down. Maybe sadness made the adults around you uncomfortable, so you learned to hide it. Maybe fear was seen as weakness, so you learned to pretend you weren't scared. There are so many things you may have internalized without realizing it.

But whatever that child felt, it was real and there was a reason for it. They were having normal, human responses to difficult situations. Their feelings were information, not problems to be solved.

Feeling Validation Exercise:

Think about a specific difficult experience from your childhood. Now imagine that child coming to you and expressing exactly how they felt about it: angry, sad, scared, confused, whatever comes up.

Instead of trying to talk them out of their feelings or fix them, just validate them. You might say things like:

- *Of course you felt scared, that was scary*
- *It makes sense that you were angry, that wasn't fair*
- *You have every right to feel sad about that*
- *Your feelings are important and valid*

Practice: Write out a conversation between you, as your adult self, and your younger self in which you validate whatever feelings come up about a particular experience and offer support.

Conversation with my younger self:

Me Now:

____

____

Little Me:

Me Now:

Little Me:

Me Now:

Little Me:

Me Now:

Little Me:

Me Now:

What I notice t in my thoughts and/or body:

Creating safety in your body

Connecting with your younger self isn't just a mental exercise, it's a whole-body experience. Trauma and fear live in the body, and healing happens there too.

As you do this work, you might notice physical sensations: tightness in your chest, tension in your shoulders, a pit in your stomach. This is your body's way of communicating. It's been holding these experiences for a long time.

Body Compassion Practice:

Take a moment to scan your body from head to toe. Notice any areas of tension, pain, or discomfort. Instead of trying to change or fix these sensations, just acknowledge them with gentleness and kindness.

You might place your hand on an area that feels tight and say something like:

- *I notice you're holding tension. Thank you for trying to protect me.*
- *I see you're in pain. I'm here with you.*
- *You've been working so hard to keep me safe. You can rest now.*

This isn't about making the sensations go away, it's about changing your relationship with them. Instead of fighting your body's responses, you're offering understanding, compassion, and safety.

Breathing Practice for Safety:

If breathing exercises are challenging for you, you can simply spend a few moments noticing your breath, feeling the inhalations and exhalations until you're ready for more.

Here's a simple breathing technique you can use anytime you're feeling overwhelmed or disconnected:

1. Breathe in slowly through your nose for a count of 4
2. Hold your breath gently for a count of 4
3. Exhale slowly through your mouth for a count of 6
4. Rest for a count of 2
5. Repeat 3-5 times

The longer exhale helps activate your nervous system's relaxation response. You're telling your body "It's safe to relax."

Daily Body Check-ins:

For the next week, I invite you to practice checking in with your body at least once a day. You might set a gentle reminder on your phone or do it at the same time each day (like right after you wake up or before bed).

Simply scan your body and notice what's there without trying to change it. If you find tension or discomfort, practice breathing into this space and offering it some compassion.

Space for daily body check-in:

The ongoing relationship

This is important to understand: connecting with your younger self isn't a one-time event or practice. It's the beginning of an ongoing relationship. That child has been waiting for your attention for a long time, and they deserve more than a quick visit.

Think of it like building trust with any relationship. You show up consistently, you listen without trying to fix, you offer comfort when it's needed, and you prove through your actions that you're safe and reliable.

Some days, your younger self might need reassurance. Other days, they might need to be heard. Sometimes they might just need to know you're there, even if they can't quite trust you yet.

Practice: This week, try to check in with your younger self at least once a day. It doesn't have to be a long, formal meditation. It might just be a moment of placing your hand on your heart and asking "How are you doing, little one?" or "What do you need right now?"

Trust whatever comes up. Sometimes the answer will be clear. Sometimes it will be confusing. Sometimes there might be no answer at all. That's all okay.

Space for daily check-ins with younger self:

Moving forward with compassion

As we prepare to move into the next section, please remember - there is no right or perfect way to do this. You don't have to feel overwhelming love for your younger self right away. In fact, you likely won't... *yet*. You don't have to have profound insights or transformative experiences.

What matters is that you're showing up. You're willing to practice a different way of being with yourself. You're choosing compassion over criticism, connection over isolation.

The child you were has been waiting for this, for someone to see them, to believe them, to offer them the care they deserved all along. That someone is you.

Closing Reflection: What's one thing you want your younger self to know as you complete this section?

What I want my younger self to know:

Commitment: What's one small way you can continue practicing compassion with yourself this week?

My commitment to practicing compassion:

Remember: Building a relationship with your younger self is a practice, not a performance. Be patient with yourself as you learn this new way of being. Every moment of compassion matters, no matter how small.

Part 3 - Releasing What Was Never Yours

If you've been practicing the compassion work from Part 2, you might be noticing something interesting: the more you connect with your younger self, the more clearly you can see that what that child was carrying was never theirs to carry.

As we talked about before, children are natural meaning-makers. When something goes wrong in their world, they don't think "This adult is struggling" or "This is about their issues." They think "This must be about me." They take on responsibility, blame, and shame that belongs to the adults around them.

Today, we're going to practice something that helps heal all the parts of yourself at the deepest levels: giving back what was never yours to begin with.

Take a moment to settle in. Place your feet flat on the floor, feel your body in your chair. Take three deep breaths, letting each exhale be a little longer than the inhale. As you breathe, imagine creating a bubble of safety around yourself... a space where you can explore without judgment, where you can feel whatever comes up.

The weight you've been carrying

Think about a heavy backpack filled with rocks. Now imagine that as a small child, adults kept putting their rocks in your backpack: their anger, their disappointment, their problems, their inability to cope. But because you were a child, you thought those rocks became yours and your responsibility to manage. You've been carrying them ever since.

The rocks might look like:

- *I'm responsible for everyone else's happiness*
- *If I'm good enough, people won't leave me*
- *I caused the problems in my family*
- *I'm too much/too sensitive/too needy*
- *I have to earn love through performance*
- *Other people's needs matter more than mine*
- *I'm fundamentally flawed, broken, or bad*
- *If I were better/different I wouldn't be hurt*

Reflection: What rocks have you been carrying in your backpack? What beliefs about yourself feel heavy and burdensome?

Some rocks I've been carrying:

The child's logic

Here's something that might help you understand why you picked up these rocks in the first place: children need to believe their caregivers are good and safe. It's a survival mechanism. If a child believes their parent is dangerous or unable to care for them, that's terrifying, because they're completely dependent on that parent.

So instead, children make themselves the problem. If mom is angry, it's because I was bad. If dad drinks, it's because I'm stressful. If they fight, it's because I'm too much trouble. If they leave, it's because I'm not lovable enough.

This logic makes perfect sense for a child's brain. They're trying to maintain the belief that their caregivers are safe and good, which means making themselves responsible for everything that goes wrong.

But the truth is you were never, could never be responsible for the adults' inability to handle their own emotions, problems, or lives. You were just a child trying to survive in the world they created.

The primary mechanisms are the same whether the wound comes from a parent or other trusted adult. What you said to yourself will change based on the circumstances.

Compassionate Reframe Exercise:

Think of a specific situation where you blamed yourself as a child. Now take a deep breath and ask yourself: If you saw any child in this exact situation, would you blame them? What would a caring adult want that child to understand about what happened?

The situation I blamed myself for:

What I'd want the child to understand/what the child deserves to know:

Now try to allow yourself to feel the care, understanding, and support you'd offer the child. That truth applies to you too. You were that child. And that child needs to *feel* the care and understanding they deserved all along.

Understanding shame vs. guilt

Before we go further, let's talk about the difference between shame and guilt. While often used interchangeably, it's important to understand the differences. They are not the same and their impact on us makes a world of difference.

Guilt is a natural response when we've done something we don't feel good about. Whether it was wrong, bad, or something that hurt someone. The focus is on the behavior: something we did or didn't do, allowing for an opportunity for corrective action if/when necessary. It's something we can learn from.

Shame, however, is about ***who we believe we are***. It's not that we did something bad or made a mistake that hurt someone. It's that we are bad. It's that we are unworthy of love, friendship, or connection which led to making the mistake. It stems from long-held beliefs of being unworthy or fundamentally flawed. Shame is never helpful. Its only purpose is to reinforce the false beliefs.

It's likely that most of what you've been carrying isn't primarily guilt, it's shame. It can be hard to tell the difference much of the time because when shame is present, for any reason, it immediately comes to the surface at the slightest hint of guilt.

Remember, shame is always a lie. You are not bad. You are not fundamentally flawed. You are not unworthy of love.

The shame you carry was created when you internalized the message that you were responsible for things that were never your responsibility. It's like a toxic byproduct of the survival strategy your child brain used.

Before moving on to this next practice, please stay mindful of what is happening in your body. Shame can create a powerful physiological response. It can lead us to extremes of thoughts, feelings, or behaviors.

Please remember, the shame you carry has never been yours and it's safe, and beyond time, to lay it down.

Shame Inventory:

Complete these sentences, letting whatever comes up be there:

I feel ashamed when I...

____

____

____

____

____

____

I feel ashamed about being...

I feel ashamed that I...

Now, for each thing you wrote, ask yourself: “Is this really about me, or is this shame I picked up from someone else’s inability to handle their own stuff?” You can also ask: “Is what I wrote something I think someone I love should feel ashamed of in the same circumstance?”

The blame release practice

This is a powerful practice, so go slowly and be gentle with yourself. You might want to do this exercise multiple times, focusing on different situations or relationships.

Step 1: Identify the Blame

Think of a specific situation where you've been blaming yourself. The following are a few possible examples. Your situation might look quite different.

- Your parents' divorce
- A parent's drinking or mental health issues
- Being abused or neglected
- Your family's financial struggles
- A parent's anger or emotional unavailability
- Being bullied or rejected

Write down the situation and what you've been blaming yourself for:

The situation:

What I've been blaming myself for:

Step 2: See the Child

Now imagine that child - you at that age - standing in front of you. Really see them. See their size, their innocence, their complete dependence on the adults around them.

Ask yourself: Could this child have prevented what happened? Could they have been responsible for the adults' choices and reactions?

Step 3: Speak the Truth

Speak directly to that child (you can do this out loud or in writing):

"Little one, what happened was not your fault. You were not responsible for __________. You were just a child. The adults made their own choices, and those choices were about them, not about you. You could never be responsible for what they did."

What I'd say to a child to help them know they're not responsible:

____

____

____

____

____

____

Step 4: Give It Back

Now imagine that blame as something physical you can hold, like a heavy stone or a thick, suffocating blanket. Picture yourself giving it back to where it belongs by handing it back to the adults who put it on you or simply releasing it into the universe.

As you give it back, you might say: "*This was never mine to carry. I give this back to you. I am not responsible for your choices, your emotions, or your inability to cope.*"

What I want to say to leave the responsibility where it has always belonged:

Step 5: Lean into the Lightness

Notice what it feels like to not carry that blame anymore. If that feels unattainable right now, try imagining what it might feel like if you no longer carried that blame or shame. Even if it's just for a moment, let yourself feel the relief of not being responsible for something that was never yours.

What I notice when I imagine releasing this blame:

Body-based release

Sometimes responsibility, blame, and shame get stored in our bodies, and we need to release them physically as well as emotionally.

Shaking Practice:

Stand up and start shaking your hands gently. Then let the shaking move up your arms, into your shoulders, your torso, down into your legs and feet. Let your whole body shake for 30 seconds to a minute. Animals do this naturally after escaping from danger, they shake to release the stored energy.

As you shake, you might imagine shaking off the blame and shame that doesn't belong to you. When you're done, stand still and notice how your body feels.

What came up for me in thoughts or sensations:

____

____

____

____

____

____

Breathing Release:

Sit comfortably and take a deep breath in. As you breathe in, imagine gathering up all the blame and shame in your body. Hold your breath for a moment, then exhale forcefully through your mouth, imagining you're breathing out everything that doesn't belong to you... *that never has.*

Do this 5-10 times, really using your exhalation to release what you've been carrying.

Writing Release:

Sometimes we need to write out, with pen and paper, what we're releasing.

Write a letter to the sense of responsibility or shame you've been carrying. Tell it that you're done carrying it, that it doesn't belong to you, and that you're choosing to let it go. When you're done, you can tear up the letter, burn it safely, or bury it: whatever feels like a meaningful symbol of release for you.

Space for writing to what I'm releasing:

Building new patterns

An interesting thing about releasing old patterns: nature fills every vacuum. If you're going to stop carrying responsibility and shame that was never yours, you need to practice holding something else instead: like truth, compassion, and healthy responsibility.

Old Pattern → New Pattern Examples:

Old Pattern: "When someone is upset, I immediately assume it's my fault and try to fix it."

New Pattern: "When someone is upset, I can ask if they want support, but I remember that I cannot be responsible for how they feel. And, there is a significant possibility that their upset has nothing to do with me."

Old Pattern: "I say yes to everything because I'm afraid people will leave me if I set boundaries."

New Pattern: "I can say no to requests that don't work for me, knowing that people who truly care about me will respect my boundaries."

Old Pattern: "I criticize myself harshly when I make mistakes because I learned that being perfect keeps me safe."

New Pattern: "When I make mistakes, I can talk to myself the way I would talk to a good friend, with understanding and encouragement."

Your New Patterns:

Think about one responsibility, blame, or shame pattern you're ready to release. What would a healthier pattern look like?

Old pattern I'm ready to release:

New pattern I want to practice:

What would help me remember this new pattern:

The ongoing practice

Releasing what was never yours isn't a one-time event, it's an ongoing practice. You might find that blame and shame try to sneak back in, especially in stressful situations. That's normal through this journey.

When you notice old patterns coming back, you can:

1. Pause and take a breath
2. Ask yourself "Is this really mine to carry?"
3. Remind yourself of the truth: "I was just a child. This wasn't my fault."
4. Consciously choose to release it again
5. Practice your new, healthier pattern

Daily Practice for the Week:

Each day, practice identifying one thing you're carrying that isn't yours. It might be big or small: guilt about a conversation, responsibility for someone else's mood, shame about a childhood memory.

Practice giving it back. You can use the formal practice above, or just take a moment to say "This isn't mine." and imagine releasing it.

Space for daily release practice:

Rewriting your story

When you start releasing what was never yours, you get to rewrite your story. Instead of "I was a bad child who caused problems," you get to write "I was a child who was trying to survive in a difficult situation."

Instead of "I'm responsible for everyone else's happiness," you get to write "I'm responsible for my choices and responses, and others are responsible for theirs."

Instead of "I'm fundamentally flawed," you get to write "I'm a human being who is worthy of love and care, exactly as I am."

Story Rewriting Exercise:

Think about one core belief about yourself that you know came from childhood blame or shame. Write the old story, then write the new story based on truth and compassion.

Old story I've been telling myself:

____

____

____

____

____

New story based on truth and compassion:

____

____

____

____

____

What it feels like to consider this new story:

Moving forward lighter

As we complete this section, I want you to know that releasing what was never yours is one of the most loving things you can do - for yourself and for the child you were. Every piece of responsibility and shame you let go of creates more space for truth, compassion, genuine connection, and freedom.

You might not feel completely free from these old patterns *yet*, and that's okay. You can't change a lifetime of beliefs and patterns in the time it takes to journey through this workbook.

Healing happens in layers. Each time you practice releasing what isn't yours, you're building new neural pathways, teaching your body and mind a different way of being.

The child you were deserves to be free from the weight they never should have carried. And you, the adult you are now, deserves to live without that burden too.

Closing Reflection:

What feels different in my body after doing this work:

What I want to remember about releasing what was never mine:

One thing I'm committed to letting go of:

Remember: Releasing old patterns is a process that requires practice, not perfection. Be patient with yourself as you learn to carry only what is truly yours. Every moment of releasing is an act of love for the child you were and the adult you continue to become as you heal.

Part 4 - Meeting Your Child with Care

You've done some incredible work to get here. You've looked at your story from a different perspective, practiced connecting with compassion, and begun releasing what was never yours to carry. Now comes what might be the most transformative part of this journey: learning to actively care for the child you were - not just once, but as an ongoing way of honoring and healing all the parts of yourself.

This isn't about going backward or *staying stuck in the past*. This is about finally *seeing* the child within and giving that child the consistent, loving care they deserved all along. There's something beautiful that happens in this moment: when you care for your inner child, you're not just healing the past, you're healing the adult who has lived all these years with that child inside still carrying the backpack, worn down, exhausted, and unable to set it down.

Let's start by checking in with your body. Take a moment to notice how you're feeling right now. Are you excited? Nervous? Tired? Whatever you're feeling... honor it. Remember, there are no right or wrong feelings.

Place one hand on your heart and one on your belly. Take three slow breaths, imagining that you're breathing care, safety, and acceptance into your body.

The practice of care

When we talk about caring for your inner child, we're talking about something very practical and real. Think about how you naturally care for any child you love. You:

- Pay attention to their needs and feelings
- Offer comfort when they're upset
- Celebrate their joys and accomplishments
- Protect them from harm when you can
- Create predictable routines that help them feel safe
- Speak to them with kindness and patience
- Validate their experiences without trying to fix everything
- Show up consistently, even when it's hard

Your inner child needs these same things. They need you to notice them, to respond to their needs, to protect them from internal criticism, judgment, and shame and to show up with the same reliability you'd offer any child in your care.

Reflection: Think about someone who cared for you or treated you well, even if only for a brief moment or moment in time: maybe a grandparent, teacher, friend, or parent of a friend. If no one comes to mind, consider a character from a book or movie you found comforting or wished you had in your life. Whether real or imagined, what does that care feel like? What do they do that makes you feel safe and valued?

What good care feels like to me:

What that person did that made me feel cared for:

Creating internal safety

Before your inner child can fully trust you, they need to know that you're a safe person to be around. This means creating internal safety, a sense that it's okay to feel, to have needs, to be vulnerable. It means they can trust that you have the capacity to hold it.

Think about what makes a child feel safe with an adult:

- The adult is predictable and consistent
- The adult doesn't react with anger or judgment when the child shares feelings
- The adult follows through on what they say they'll do
- The adult protects the child from being overwhelmed
- The adult creates boundaries that keep the child safe

You can create this same safety for your inner child.

Internal Safety Assessment:

As you read through and rate the statements below, you may notice a quick response that says *of course they're safe*. I'd like to invite you to consider how likely it may be that when a part of you feels scared or makes a mistake, that you'd honor that vs dismiss it, judge it, or try to talk yourself out of it. When that happens, there is a lack of safety, for you both.

Rate how safe your inner child feels with you in these areas (1 = not safe at all, 5 = very safe)

It's safe for me to feel sad or scared: ____/5

It's safe for me to have needs: ____/5

It's safe for me to make mistakes: ____/5

It's safe for me to be angry: ____/5

It's safe for me to be excited or happy: ____/5

It's safe for me to ask for help: ____/5

It's safe for me to rest: ____/5

Creating Safety Practices:

For areas where you scored 3 or below, what would help create more safety?

Daily check-ins: The foundation of care

Just like you might check in with a child throughout the day, "How are you feeling?" "What do you need?" "Are you okay?" - your inner child needs regular check-ins from you.

This isn't about having long, complex conversations with yourself or having to have all the answers. It's about developing the habit of paying attention to your internal world with the same care you'd give to any child you love.

Simple Daily Check-in Practice:

Several times throughout the day, pause and ask yourself:

- *How am I feeling right now?*
- *What does my inner child need?*
- *Is there anything I'm carrying that's too heavy?*
- *What would feel caring right now?*

Trust whatever comes up. Sometimes the answer will be "I need a break." Sometimes it'll be "I need encouragement." Or, sometimes it might simply be "I need a hug and to know I matter."

Morning check-in:

Before you start your day, take a moment to connect with your inner child. You might place your hand on your heart and ask:

"Good morning, little one. How are you feeling about today? Is there anything you need from me to feel safe and cared for?"

Evening check-in:

Before you go to sleep, check in again:

"How did today go for you? What was hard? What was good? What do you need from me tonight?"

Practice Space - Daily Check-ins:

Morning check-in notes:

Evening check-in notes:

Providing comfort and reassurance

One of the most important things you can do for your inner child is to offer comfort when they're struggling. This is about learning to be your own source of soothing and reassurance.

Comfort Practices:

Physical Comfort:

- Wrap yourself in a soft or weighted blanket
- Hold a warm cup of tea or coffee
- Take a warm bath or shower
- Give yourself a gentle self-hug
- Use a heating pad or soft pillow

Emotional Comfort:

- Speak to yourself in a gentle, caring voice
- Validate your feelings: "Of course you're scared. This is scary."
- Offer reassurance: "You're safe now. I'm here with you."
- Remind yourself of your worth: "You deserve love and care."

Spiritual/Energetic Comfort:

- Spend time in nature
- Light a candle or burn incense
- Listen to soothing music
- Practice gentle movement or stretching
- Meditate or find stillness in whatever way feels right

Comfort Menu:

Create a personalized list of things that do (or may) help you feel comforted and cared for:

When I'm sad, this helps me feel better:

When I'm scared, this helps me feel safe:

When I'm angry, this helps me feel understood:

When I'm overwhelmed, this helps me feel grounded:

The Inner Caregiver Voice

Many of us have a strong critical voice, a voice that judges, criticizes, and points out everything we're doing *wrong*. But we can also develop an inner caregiver: a voice that offers the same kind of loving guidance and support you'd give to any child you care about.

Inner Critic vs. Inner Caregiver:

Inner Critic says: "You're such an idiot for making that mistake."

Inner Caregiver says: "That was a tough situation. You did the best you could with what you knew then."

Inner Critic says: "You're being too sensitive. Get over it."

Inner Caregiver says: "Your feelings make sense. It's okay to feel hurt by that."

Inner Critic says: "You should be able to handle this. Everyone else can."

Inner Caregiver says: "This is really hard and it's not true that *everyone* else can. It's okay to need support."

Developing Your Inner Caregiver:

Think about how you would talk to a child you love who was going through what you've gone or are going through. What would your voice sound like? What would you say?

When I'm struggling, my inner caregiver might say:

When I make a mistake, my inner caregiver might say:

When I'm scared, my inner caregiver might say:

Creating rituals of care

Children thrive on predictable rituals that help them feel safe and cared for. Your inner child needs these too. These don't have to be elaborate. Simple, consistent acts of care can be incredibly powerful.

Examples of Care Rituals:

Morning rituals:

- A few minutes of gentle stretching
- Drinking your coffee or tea mindfully
- Identifying and writing three things you're grateful for
- Looking in the mirror and saying something kind

Evening rituals:

- A warm bath with candles or soothing routine
- Reading something comforting

- Gentle self-massage
- Reviewing the day with compassion

Weekly rituals:

- A nature walk
- Creating something with your hands
- Cooking a favorite meal
- Spending time with people who care about you

Monthly rituals:

- Doing something creative just for fun
- Visiting a place that feels peaceful
- Buying yourself flowers or a small gift
- Having a day with no obligations

Your Care Rituals:

What daily ritual would feel caring to my inner child:

What weekly ritual would feel nurturing:

What monthly ritual would feel special:

Protecting your inner child

Part of caring for your inner child means protecting them from things that are harmful or overwhelming. This might mean setting boundaries with other people, but it also means setting boundaries with yourself.

External Protection:

- Limiting time with people who are consistently critical or draining
- Saying no to commitments that feel overwhelming
- Creating physical spaces that feel safe and nurturing
- Being selective about what media you consume

Internal Protection:

- Interrupting self-critical thoughts
- Not forcing yourself to 'get over' things before you're ready
- Giving yourself permission to have needs and feelings
- Protecting your energy and not over-extending yourself

Protection Practice:

What does my inner child need protection from?

What boundaries would help create more safety?

What would it look like to protect my inner child this week?

Building trust through consistency

Trust is built through small, consistent actions over time. Your inner child needs to know that you're not going to abandon them, criticize them, or dismiss their needs like others might have done.

This means:

- Following through on promises you make to yourself
- Showing up for your check-ins even when you're busy
- Responding to your inner child's... and your adult, needs with care, not impatience
- Being gentle with yourself when you make mistakes
- Consistently choosing care over criticism

Trust-Building Commitments:

What small, daily commitment can I make to my inner child?

What weekly commitment feels manageable and caring?

How will I respond when I mess up or forget?

Working with difficult emotions

Sometimes when you start caring for your inner child, difficult emotions come up. This is normal. That child has been waiting a long time to be seen and cared for, and they might have a lot of feelings about it.

You might notice:

- Sadness about what you missed
- Anger about how you were treated
- Fear about trusting this new relationship
- Guilt about focusing on yourself
- Resistance to being vulnerable

All of these feelings are welcome. Part of caring for your inner child means making space for whatever emotions arise.

When difficult emotions come up:

- Don't try to fix or change the emotion – just be present with it.
- Validate the feeling – "Of course you're sad. You missed out on a lot."
- Offer comfort – use your comfort practices
- Remember it's temporary – emotions are like waves, they rise and fall naturally
- Seek support if needed or desired – sometimes we all need help processing big emotions

Emotion Practice:

What difficult emotions have come up as I've navigated this work?

What does my inner child need when these emotions arise?

How can I offer comfort during difficult emotional moments?

Creating joyful experiences

Caring for your inner child means giving them opportunities for joy, play, and delight, perhaps for the first time. Some people have clear memories of childhood joy, while others may need to discover what brings their inner child happiness now. What brought you joy as a child? What makes you laugh? What brings you lightness now?

Rediscovering Joy:

Things that bring me joy or make me laugh:

What would my inner child want to experience:

New things I'd like to try that might bring joy:

Weekly Joy Practice:

Commit to doing one thing each week that brings your inner child joy. You may have difficulty identifying something. You may have difficulty *feeling* joy initially. If this is true for you, think of it as something you've wanted to try, maybe even as a child. Or, consider something that has the possibility to bring joy, peace, or laughter. The following are just some examples. Do what makes your heart happy.

- Playing with art supplies
- Dancing to music you love
- Spending time in nature
- Watching a favorite movie
- Playing a game
- Cooking something delicious
- Reading for pleasure

The ongoing relationship

Remember: caring for your inner child is not a project to complete, it's a relationship to nurture. Some days will be easier than others. Some days your inner child will feel trusting and open. Other days they might feel scared or resistant.

That's all normal. What matters is that you keep showing up. What matters is that you're learning to be the consistent, caring presence that child always needed.

Weekly Care Plan:

For the next week, commit to these care practices. *You don't have to be perfect, just make an effort.*

Daily:

A few days throughout the week:

Weekly:

Progress Check:

How is my relationship with my inner child changing?

What feels different in my daily life?

What do I want to remember about caring for my inner child?

Moving forward with love

As we complete this section, I want you to know that learning to care for your inner child is one of the most revolutionary things you can do. In a world that often tells us to "get over" our past, to be independent, to not need anyone, you're choosing something radically different: you're choosing to be the caring presence the child within ***always*** deserved.

This care you're learning to give yourself will naturally overflow into other aspects of your life. When you know how to nurture your own inner child, you become more patient, more compassionate, and more able to show up for yourself in ways that are healing to you both.

The child you were is not a burden to carry, they're a gift to cherish. They hold your strength, resilience, courage, creativity, your wonder, and your capacity for joy. They deserve your love, your attention, and your care.

Closing Commitment:

My promise to my inner child:

How I want to show up for myself moving forward:

Remember: This is a practice of love, not perfection. Every moment of care you offer your inner child matters. Every time you choose compassion over criticism, you're healing not just the past, but creating a more loving present and future.

Part 5 - Living from Freedom

You've traveled a remarkable journey to get to this moment in time and healing. You've begun to connect with your inner child through compassion, release what was never yours to carry, and develop practices for caring for yourself with the same tenderness you'd offer any child you love.

Now comes the most incredible part: learning to live from this place of healing. This isn't about becoming someone new, it's about becoming more fully yourself. It's about living from the freedom that comes when you're no longer carrying the weight of old wounds, when you're no longer trying to prove your worth, when you feel deeply rooted in the truth that you are, *and always have been*, enough exactly as you are.

Living from freedom doesn't mean you'll never struggle again. It means that when you do, you'll show up differently for yourself and the child within who may feel some familiar feelings. You'll meet the struggle with more self-compassion, more internal resources, and more trust in your resilience. It means you'll be able to show up in your life and relationships from a place of grounded authenticity rather than survival.

Take a moment to settle into your body. Feel your feet on the ground, your body in your chair. Take three slow breaths, and as you breathe, imagine breathing in possibility. What would it feel like to live from a place of genuine freedom, without the weight of that backpack? What would be different? Just let yourself wonder.

What freedom feels like

Freedom isn't the absence of stress or problems, it's the presence of choice. When you're living from a grounded, healed place you have options that weren't available when you were stuck in old patterns of survival and protection.

Freedom feels like:

- Being able to feel your emotions without being overwhelmed by them
- Having conflicts without losing yourself or believing you're fundamentally flawed
- Setting boundaries without feeling guilty or terrified of abandonment
- Making mistakes without it meaning you're a failure as a person
- Being able to receive love and care without feeling like you have to earn it
- Trusting your own perceptions and feelings
- Being able to be present with others without losing yourself
- Having access to your full range of emotions - including joy, excitement, and peace

- Knowing that you can handle whatever comes up because you trust in yourself
- Feeling the safety and lightness of no longer holding shame that was never yours

Reflection: What would freedom feel like for you specifically? What would be different in your daily life?

Freedom would feel like:

In my daily life, I would notice:

Living from your adult self

One of the most beautiful aspects of this healing work is that you get to (re)discover who you are. The real you, under the old wounds. The you that existed before your experiences and the world taught you something different. You get to reconnect to the wholeness that has always existed within you.

Your adult self has access to:

- **Wisdom** - you can see situations more clearly, without the distortion of old trauma
- **Choice** - you can respond rather than react
- **Boundaries** - you can say yes and no from a place of self-respect
- **Creativity** - you can access your natural gifts and talents

- **Connection** - you can form genuine relationships based on who you are, not who you think you need to be
- **Resilience** - you can handle challenges because you trust your own capacity

Adult Self Exploration:

When I'm operating from my adult self (not from old wounds or beliefs), I am:

____

____

____

____

____

My adult self's natural gifts and strengths are:

____

____

____

____

____

My adult self values:

____

____

____

____

____

My adult self dreams of:

Navigating challenges from a healed place

Living from freedom doesn't mean you won't face difficulties. Life will still bring loss, disappointment, conflict, and uncertainty. But you'll navigate these challenges differently when you're operating from a place of inner healing.

Old Pattern vs. New Response:

When someone criticizes me:

Old pattern: Immediately believe they're right, feel shame, either collapse or get defensive

New response: Listen for any valid feedback while remembering that their opinion doesn't define my worth

When I make a mistake:

Old pattern: Spiral into shame or self-criticism, feel like a failure, withdraw from others

New response: Feel disappointed but not devastated, learn from it, ask for support if needed

When someone is upset with me:

Old pattern: Panic, take full responsibility, do anything to fix it immediately

New response: Stay present with their emotion while maintaining my own center, respond thoughtfully

When I'm feeling overwhelmed:

Old pattern: Push through, criticize myself for not being stronger, isolate

New response: Acknowledge the overwhelm, break things down into smaller steps, reach out for support

Your Challenge Navigation:

Think about a specific challenge you're facing or often face. How might you handle it differently from a place of healing?

The challenge:

____

____

____

____

____

How I typically handle it:

____

____

____

____

____

How I might handle it from a place of freedom:

What support would help me respond from my healed place:

Creating authentic relationships

One of the most profound changes that happens when you heal your inner child is that your relationships become more authentic. You no longer need to pretend to be someone else to think you could be loved, you can show up as yourself and trust that people will accept and appreciate who you are.

Authentic relating means:

- Being honest about your feelings and needs
- Setting boundaries when something doesn't feel right
- Asking for help when you need it
- Saying no without elaborate justifications
- Sharing your true opinions and interests
- Being vulnerable when it feels safe and appropriate
- Choosing relationships based on mutual respect and care
- Ending relationships that consistently drain or harm you

Relationship Inventory:

Relationships where I feel most authentic:

Relationships where I feel like I have to pretend or perform:

What would change if I brought more authenticity to my relationships:

What fears come up about being more authentic:

How can I support myself in being more authentic:

Honoring your needs without guilt

Children who grew up in difficult circumstances often learned that their needs were inconvenient, too much, or not important. Living from freedom means reclaiming your right to have needs and to honor them without guilt.

Types of needs:

- **Physical needs:** Rest, nutrition, movement, comfort, safety
- **Emotional needs:** Love, acceptance, understanding, validation, fun
- **Mental needs:** Stimulation, learning, creativity, problem-solving
- **Spiritual/Energetic needs:** Connection, meaning, purpose, peace
- **Social needs:** Belonging, friendship, intimacy, community

Needs Practice:

What I need right now:

What I need more of in my life:

What I need less of in my life:

How I can honor these needs:

What gets in the way of honoring my needs:

Trusting Your Inner Wisdom

One of the most beautiful gifts of healing is that you get to trust yourself again. You learn that your feelings, perceptions, and instincts are valid and important. You don't need external validation to know what's true for you.

Inner wisdom shows up as:

- Gut feelings about people and situations
- Knowing what feels right or wrong for you
- Intuitive understanding of what you need
- Creative insights and inspirations
- Physical sensations that guide you
- Dreams and symbolic understanding
- Natural knowing about timing and decisions

Trusting Yourself Practice:

A time when I trusted my inner wisdom and it served me well:

Areas where I still doubt myself:

What would help me trust my inner wisdom more:

How my inner wisdom typically communicates with me:

Maintaining your healing

Healing isn't a destination; it's an ongoing practice. There will be times when old patterns resurface, when old wounds or beliefs come to the surface, when you need to return to the basics of caring for your inner child... *and your adult self.* This doesn't mean you've failed; it means you're human, experiencing the natural progression of healing and life.

Maintenance practices:

- Regular check-ins with your inner child
- Consistent self-care that nourishes you
- Boundaries that protect your energy and time
- Relationships that support your authentic self
- Creative expression that brings you joy
- Movement and activities that help you feel embodied
- Professional support when needed

Your Maintenance Plan:

Daily practices that keep me connected to my healthier, embodied self:

Weekly practices that support my ongoing healing:

Monthly practices that help me stay on track:

Warning signs that I need to focus more on my healing:

Support systems I can access when needed:

Ripples of your healing

When you're no longer using all your energy to survive, protect, or please, something shifts. The space once filled with fear and self-protection opens to authenticity, creativity, and connection. Your healing doesn't just change your inner world; it ripples outward in ways you may not even see. The way you love, create, and show up becomes a reflection of the wholeness you've reclaimed.

Your healing contributes to:

- Breaking cycles of trauma in your family and your life
- Creating healthy relationships that nourish you
- Seeing and valuing yourself more fully
- Creating environments where you and those around you feel safe
- Expressing your authentic self through your choices and actions
- Showing others that healing is possible
- Deepening compassion for every part of who you are

Embodying my healing:

You may not feel or recognize there is healing that has already happened. But it doesn't mean there haven't been many moments along the way that have and will continue to contribute to your journey. They are there, often in seemingly small shifts. Shifts that may not feel certain just yet. It's important to remember that healing is a process and a practice. Each time you practice you move further along the path. If you aren't able to identify any shifts yet, allow yourself to imagine what it might look like as you respond to the prompts below.

How has my healing changed the way I move through life:

How has my healing made me more able to access my authentic self:

What has become possible for me that once felt out of reach:

What feels authentic and meaningful to me now:

In what ways do I see my healing influencing the people or spaces around me:

How do I want to continue embodying my healing as I grow:

Living from what matters

When you're not constantly protecting yourself from old wounds, you get to choose to live according to your desires, needs, and values rather than your fears and false beliefs. You get to make decisions based on what is important to you, not what you fear might happen or what people think.

Values Clarification:

What matters most to me:

How I want to treat myself:

How I want to treat others:

How I want to be treated by others:

The kind of life I want to create:

Values and Desires in Action:

One way I can live my values and desires more fully:

One decision I can make based on my desires or values rather than my fears:

Creating a life that honors your worth

Living from freedom means creating a life that reflects your inherent worth, not a life you think you deserve based on your experiences or achievements. A life that honors who you are as a human being.

This might look like:

- Creating spaces that feel nurturing and beautiful
- Pursuing work or other endeavors that feel meaningful and aligned
- Making time for activities that bring you joy
- Caring for your body with love rather than punishment or shame
- Investing in relationships that are mutual and supportive
- Setting boundaries that protect your energy and well-being
- Following your curiosity and interests
- Taking risks that align with your desires
- Creating traditions and rituals that feel meaningful

Life Vision:

What would a life that honors my worth look like:

What would I change if I truly believed I deserve good things:

What steps can I take toward creating this life:

The ongoing journey

What you've explored in these pages is not the end of the journey. It's the beginning of living from a more attuned life. You've built a foundation that allows your healing to move with you into daily life; shaping how you care for yourself, connect with others, and move through the world as your whole self.

There will be times when you forget these practices, when old patterns resurface, when you feel disconnected from your inner child. That's normal. That's human. That's part of the journey.

When that happens, you can return to these practices. You can come back to compassion. You can remember that you are worthy of love and care. You can choose again. And each time, you return home to yourself, again and again, with more understanding... and healing.

Integration Questions:

What has been the most important learning from this workbook:

What practice(s) do I most want to continue:

What am I most excited about as I move forward:

What do I want to remember on difficult days:

Your letter to the future

As a way of completing this workbook, I'd like to invite you to write a letter to yourself, to be opened sometime in the future when you might need reminding of what you've learned and who you're becoming.

Letter to My Future Self:

Dear Future Me,

I'm writing this after completing the Inner Child Healing Workbook. Right now, I feel...

The most important thing I've learned is...

I want you to remember...

When you're struggling, please remember...

You are worthy of...

I'm proud of you for...

Keep going because...

With love and gratitude, [Your name] on [Today's date]

Final reflection

Take a moment to acknowledge yourself for showing up to this work. It takes deep courage to look at your story, to feel what you once had to hide, and to learn new ways of being. You have given yourself, and the child you once were, an extraordinary gift.

Healing invites a different way of living, one rooted in awareness, compassion, and truth. The freedom you are stepping into belongs entirely to you. Let it shape how you move through the world, how you meet yourself, and how you continue to grow.

My Commitment to the Journey:

My commitment to myself and my inner child as I move forward:

How I will honor this work:

What I want to remember always:

Remember: You are not broken. You never were. You are a human being who experienced difficult things and learned to survive. Now you get to learn to thrive and experience the freedom you've both deserved. The child you were is proud of you. The adult you're becoming deserves celebrating. Keep going. Keep growing. Keep choosing you both.

The Path Forward

As you reach the end of this workbook, take a moment to acknowledge what you've done. You've looked at your story with courage. You've felt feelings that may have been buried for years. You've practiced meeting yourself with compassion instead of judgment. You've begun to release what was never yours to carry.

This is sacred work. This is courageous work. And you've done it. The child within is both grateful and so very proud of you.

What Freedom Looks Like

Healing from childhood wounds doesn't mean you'll never feel pain again or that you'll somehow become "perfect". It means you'll know, deep in your bones, that you are worthy of love and care, not because of what you do or achieve, but simply because you exist.

It means when that old familiar shame or self-criticism arises, you'll recognize it as the echo of old wounds, not the truth of who you are. You'll have tools to comfort yourself, to speak to yourself with compassion, to remember that the child in you deserves gentle care.

Freedom looks like trusting your own feelings, setting boundaries without guilt, and allowing yourself to take up space in the world. It looks like authentic relationships built on honesty rather than the exhausting work of trying to be who you think others want you to be.

Most importantly, freedom looks like coming home to yourself - the real you, the one who was always whole and worthy of love.

The Journey Continues

This workbook may be ending, but your journey of healing continues. There will be days when you believe in possibility and you feel strong and connected to your worth. There will be other days when the old patterns or beliefs creep back in. Both are part of the process.

Remember: healing isn't linear. You might return to these pages when you need reminding. You might find new meanings in exercises you've done before. Through it all, you'll discover that what once felt impossible now feels natural.

Keep going. Keep practicing. Keep choosing compassion over criticism, connection over isolation, truth over the stories that once kept you small.

The child in you is always worth coming back to. Always worth caring for. Always worth fighting for. And is so grateful you chose this journey and is incredibly proud of who you've become.

A Poem for the Child You Were

You were small, with dreams bigger than your body and a heart that hadn't yet learned to build walls around itself.

You deserved soft voices and gentle hands, laughter that filled rooms and safety that never wavered.

You deserved to be celebrated for your curiosity, your questions, your beautiful, wild aliveness.

The world may have taught you to shrink, to apologize for your needs, to carry blame that wasn't yours.

But please know: You were never too much. You were never not enough. You were exactly as you were meant to be.

You were braver than you knew, more courageous than you believed, stronger and more resilient than you imagined.

You survived. You carried hope when everything felt dark. You found ways to keep your spirit alive.

That strength is still yours. That courage is still yours. That beautiful heart is still yours. And it has lived on in the adult you became.

You are worthy of love, worthy of safety, worthy of all the tenderness you've been waiting for.

You always were. You always will be.

A commitment to yourself

Before you close this part of your journey, write a commitment... a promise to yourself and the little one inside you. A commitment to honor the work you've done by returning to the self-compassion you've connected to here. A promise to honor the truth when there is struggle and the dreams that live in your heart. It's not about perfection. It's a practice to remind you both that you deserve all that healing brings.

My promise to us both:

Thoughts, Feelings, Reflections

About the Author

Peggy Oliveira, MSW is a social worker, childhood trauma therapist, survivor, Reiki practitioner, and founder of Courageous Journeys®, a practice and platform devoted to healing childhood trauma *together*. For more than 20 years, she has supported survivors in understanding and healing the lasting impact of childhood trauma and the ways it shapes beliefs, emotions, relationships, and the sense of self.

Her work helps people return to wholeness by dismantling the false beliefs trauma and childhood wounds create, guiding survivors toward the freedom that becomes possible when fear, shame, and doubt no longer lead the way.

Through Courageous Journeys®, she offers individual mentoring, group healing experiences, and a collection of courses and tools designed to support meaningful, lasting healing. A large library of free videos on YouTube offers education, reflection, and guidance for those on their courageous journey of becoming who they were always meant to be.

To learn more, visit CourageousJourneys.com or find her on YouTube @ Peggy Oliveira, MSW.

Made in United States
Orlando, FL
31 July 2026

85153039R10083